A BOOK FOR

The Ultimate
Sea Glass Hunter!

Enjoy your sea glass
adventures!

Hello!

You have been given this book because you are part of an amazing club, known by many names including:

Sea Glass Hunters
Glunters
Sea Glassers
Beach Combers

A unique group of people who spend any free moment by the ocean, scouring the shoreline for little nuggets of history, worn by the ebb and flow of the tide.

Only fellow sea glass hunters can appreciate the feeling of pure joy when they spot that perfectly 'cooked' glass jewel in the sand.

How did it get there? Where and when did it come from?

This is a book to help you on your sea glass journey.

What will the waves bring this time?!

HOW TO USE YOUR BOOK

The joy of sea glassing is that you don't need expensive equipment or expertise.

It is something you can do alone, or with others.

You can be 4 years old, or 104!

All you need is a beach, patience and a keen eye.

Throughout the pages of this book there are examples of different things to find, alongside explanations of what they are. There are also handy tick boxes, so every time you find something new you can tick your book (and add other details if you like).

(Lyme Regis)

Like this ➡ ✓

06/08/23

Some beach finds are rare, sometimes they are valuable, and many are beautiful.
All finds are exciting!

You can often spy a fellow sea glass hunter on the beach, easily recognisable by their stoop, their eyes focused on the ground and the occasional 'happy dance' when they find a real gem!

Whether you are a total beginner or a seasoned sea glasser, there is enough to keep you searching for a lifetime!

Happy hunting!

Glorious

DEEP SMOKE GREY

DEEP ROSE GREY

☐

☐

LIGHT SMOKE GREY

WARM GREY

☐

☐

Greys

SMOKE
GREY

GREY

LIGHT
GREY

COOL
GREY

SILVER
GREY

PALE
ICE

Most grey sea glass comes from the decade
between 1915 - 1925.
The thick pieces of grey are usually over 100
years old.
The majority of grey glass was once clear glass
containing elements that react with sunlight.

Gorgeous

DARK OLIVE GREEN	DARK OLIVE YELLOW	DARK FOREST GREEN	DARK GREEN	DARK TEAL GREEN

OLIVE GREEN	MOSS GREEN	LIME GREEN	LIGHT JADE GREEN	SAGE GREEN

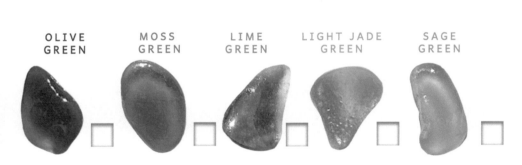

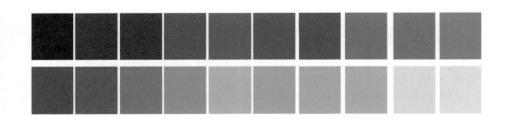

Greens

GREEN	GREEN BLUE	JADE GREEN	EMERALD GREEN	KELLY GREEN
☐	☐	☐	☐	☐

LIGHT OLIVE GREEN	UV GREEN	SOFT GREEN	PALE UV GREEN	PALE SAGE GREEN
☐	☐	☐	☐	☐

Green sea glass is one of the most common colours found on shores all over the world. It is used in many bottles we use today including fizzy drinks, wine and beer bottles. Kelly green is the most frequently found green.

Beautiful

DARK BLUE	DARK COBALT BLUE	BLUE	COBALT BLUE	CORNFLOWER BLUE

LIGHT CORNFLOWER BLUE	AQUAMARINE	AQUA BLUE	LIGHT AQUAMARINE	PASTEL BLUE

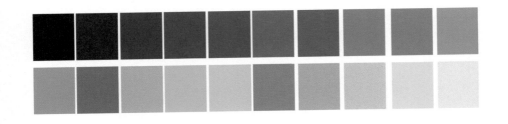

Blues

TEAL BLUE	ELECTRIC BLUE	STEEL BLUE	SKY BLUE	DEEP AQUA BLUE
☐	☐	☐	☐	☐

DARK STEEL BLUE	DEEP STEEL GREY-BLUE	PALE AQUAMARINE	PALE SKY BLUE	ICE BLUE
☐	☐	☐	☐	☐

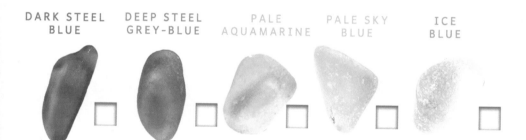

Blue sea glass is a favourite for sea glassers.
Cobalt blue glass has always been treasured and
was a sign of wealth in the 1700s.
The centre of production for blue glass tableware
was in Bristol, England.
By the 1860s blue glass was used for utilitarian
bottles, especially medicine and poison bottles.
Production of this increased by the beginning of the
20th century.

Amazing

DARK BROWN

☐

BURGUNDY

☐

DARK RED AMBER

☐

DARK AMBER

☐

MAROON

☐

DEEP ORANGE

☐

ORANGE

☐

AMBER

☐

HONEY AMBER

☐

YELLOW GOLD

☐

Ambers

CRIMSON	MAGENTA	SCARLET	RED	DEEP AMBER
☐	☐	☐	☐	☐

LIGHT YELLOW GOLD	PALE OLIVE YELLOW	OLIVE YELLOW	YELLOW	PALE YELLOW
☐	☐	☐	☐	☐

Brown sea glass is common to find. It comes from many frequently-used items such as beer, wine and medicine bottles.

Red and yellow sea glass is very difficult to find and a real prize, perhaps originating from art glass, decorative and dinnerware glass or even car and boat lights.

Stunning

TEAL

☐

LIGHT TEAL

☐

LIGHT TEAL GREY

☐

SEAFOAM

☐

Sea Foams

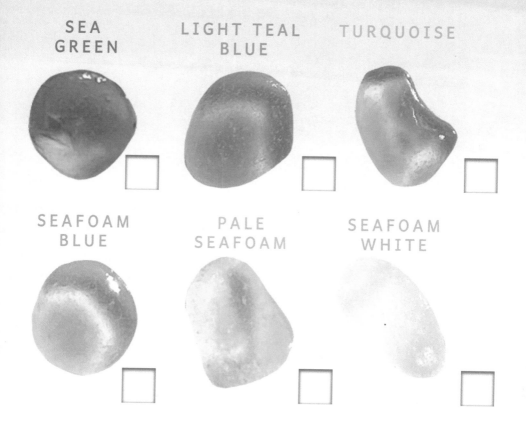

SEA GREEN

LIGHT TEAL BLUE

TURQUOISE

SEAFOAM BLUE

PALE SEAFOAM

SEAFOAM WHITE

Sea foam glass, although fairly common, is a collector's favourite due to its calming ocean shades.

The soft aqua colouring is caused by iron found in the sand used to make old bottles from the late 1800s and early 1900s.

Pretty Pinks

DARK AMETHYST	DEEP VIOLET	ROUGE PINK	AMETHYST

☐ ☐ ☐ ☐

ROSE PURPLE	DEEP PINK	PINK	PEACH

☐ ☐ ☐ ☐

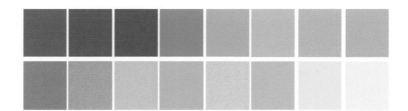

and Purples

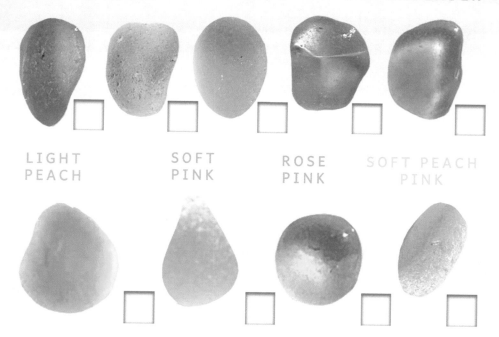

LIGHT AMETHYST	VIOLET	PALE INDIGO	LAVENDER	PALE LAVENDER
☐	☐	☐	☐	☐

LIGHT PEACH	SOFT PINK	ROSE PINK	SOFT PEACH PINK
☐	☐	☐	☐

Pale pink (peach) sea glass usually comes from 'Depression glass' made in the USA in the early 1930s.
Most lavender sea glass began as clear glass.
Between 1865 and 1920 manganese was added to glass to hide the greenish colour of the clear glass, but manganese turns lavender when exposed to UV rays in sunlight.
Purple sea glass was reserved for bishops and the monarchy and is therefore very rare to find as sea glass.

Strange

BONFIRE GLASS ☐

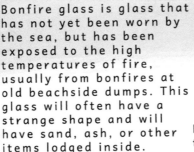

Bonfire glass is glass that has not yet been worn by the sea, but has been exposed to the high temperatures of fire, usually from bonfires at old beachside dumps. This glass will often have a strange shape and will have sand, ash, or other items lodged inside.

BONFIRE SEA GLASS ☐

Bonfire sea glass has been tumbled by the sea. Sometimes bonfire glass has two or more colours that have been melted together.

SAFETY GLASS ☐

Safety glass is also known as wire mesh or chicken wire glass. It was a low-cost fire-resistant glass, with wire mesh inlaid to prevent it from shattering. It was used in schools and factories until 2003.

MILK GLASS ☐

Milk glass is an opaque translucent glass, usually white, blue, green, pink, black or yellow. It became popular in the 1880s as a less-expensive substitute for porcelain.

UV GLASS ☐

UV glass contains uranium and was used as decorative glass from the 1800s. Production dwindled from the 1940s onwards due to the higher demand for uranium in WWII and the Cold War.
This glass glows under a black light.

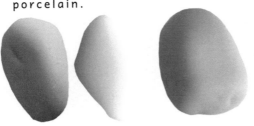

Sea Glass

PIRATE GLASS

Pirate glass appears to be black, but when held against a strong light can be a variety of colours, usually dark olive green, dark purple or amber. From the 1700s, thick black glass was used to make bottles that held alcohol and other drinks which protected the contents from breakages in rough seas. The darkness of the glass helped preserve the liquor.
It is rumoured that pirates drank from the very bottles this sea glass is made from!

TV GLASS

This two-toned grey glass is from old TV screens and is very rare to find.

SLAG GLASS

Slag glass is the by-product of the metal ore smelting process. It often looks like lumpy rocks.

DRAGON EGGS

Dragon eggs are a unique form of sea-worn slag glass, with colourful stripes, patterns and swirls. Mainly found in the North East of England, it is also known as 'galaxy glass'.

PATTERNED GLASS

Patterned glass can come from a number of sources including decorative items and privacy windows. If the pattern has indents it is likely to be from the 1820s onwards, when molten glass was poured into cast iron moulds.

Sculpted by

BOTTLE TOP RING ☐

The very top of a bottle is all that is left in these perfectly worn rings.

BOTTLE NECK ☐

Bottle necks come in many lengths and colours.

HANDLE ☐

These are often from drinking glasses, vases and jugs.

BOTTLE BOTTOM ☐

A worn disc that was once the flat base of a bottle.

PIKO ☐

A Piko, or belly button (from the Hawaiian word for naval) is the inside nubbin or outside blob seal from a glass fishing float.

MERMAID'S NIPPLE ☐

These are often exactly the same as a Piko and their names are interchangeable, however some mermaid nipples are made from a wine glass where the stem meets the base.

the Waves

VITRITE ☐

Invented in 1902, these black glass caps were used to insulate the electrical filament at the base of incandescent light bulbs. Pieces of these can be found on beaches all over the world.

KICK UP or PUSH UP ☐

Formed from the centre of the bottom of a bottle, most commonly found on wine and champagne bottles.

HEART ☐

Sometimes you can be lucky and find sea glass that has been shaped into a heart by the waves.

BOULDER ☐

Boulders are lumps of glass, sometimes bigger than a lemon! They are formed from leftover glass that was discarded by factories into the sea.

VULCANITE STOPPER ☐

Black bottle stoppers are made from a material called vulcanite or ebonite; a mixture of natural rubber, linseed oil and sulphur, made to look like ebony wood. These stoppers were often embossed with logos and were used from the 1870s to the 1970s.

GLASS BOTTLE STOPPER ☐

These beautiful glass pieces were widely used for sealing food and drink containers from the mid-19th century until the mid-20th century.
They come in many shapes, sizes and colours, most commonly whites and sea foams.

DECORATIVE CERAMIC LID ☐

A patterned, painted or glazed mushroom-shaped ceramic lid could possibly be from a tea set.

STOPPER SHARD ☐

If you find a deliberately- shaped piece of sea glass similar to these, it may have once been part of a stopper.

Sea Stoppers

PORCELAIN BEER BOTTLE STOPPER ☐

These stoppers were originally invented in 1877 and are still used on beer bottles today. They work by sealing the mouth of a bottle with a swing-away rubber seal. They would have originally had logos on the top, but this has usually been worn away by the ocean.

CHANDELIER GLASS ☐

Although it may look like a stopper shard, if you can see cut edges you may have found a piece from a chandelier.

DECORATIVE STOPPER ☐

Some glass stoppers are decorative and ornate with many differently-shaped tops. These may have belonged to perfume bottles, decanters, and apothecary bottles.

GLASS JAR LID ☐

Just like bottles, jars containing foods were also sealed with glass lids, often with a metal clamp, before the advent of screw top metal lids.

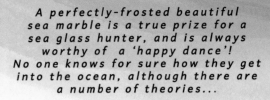

A perfectly-frosted beautiful sea marble is a true prize for a sea glass hunter, and is always worthy of a 'happy dance'! No one knows for sure how they get into the ocean, although there are a number of theories...

CODD MARBLE ☐

SEEDED MARBLE ☐

In 1870, a London inventor called Hiram Codd created a new bottle design to preserve fizzy drinks. This design used a rubber seal and a glass marble in the neck of the bottle. Once the drink was finished, the bottles were dumped (often in beachside dumps) or smashed so that children could play with the marble inside. These can still be found in Europe, especially on UK beaches.
Bottles with marbles in the neck are still made in some parts of the world.

Seeded sea glass has been deliberately thrown into the ocean to be found by future sea glass hunters.
The most common seeded glass is marbles and vase beads. Although there is no way to really know if something is seeded or not, if it is not sea-worn and frosty, it is possible that someone has left it there recently.

INDUSTRIAL 'RAILROAD' MARBLE ☐

SPRAY CAN MARBLE ☐

Industrial marbles are nicknamed 'railroad marbles' because they are commonly found near railroad tracks in the USA.
They were most likely used in the manufacturing of other glass products such as fibreglass in the early 1900s.
They come in shades of sea green and are bigger than a playing marble. Industrial marbles are usually imperfect, they often feature a rough fold line and are full of air bubbles.

If you have ever shaken a spray paint can, you will have heard it rattle. This is caused by the 'pea' which is there to mix the paint from the inside. The pea is often a glass marble made from recycled bottle glass. It is nearly always clear or plain without any pattern. They end up in the ocean after the can has rusted away.

Ocean Orbs

SEA GLASS MARBLE ☐

Colourful glass marbles were invented in Germany in the mid-1800s. By the 1900s other countries learned how to create them, and by the 1920s and 30s marbles were hugely popular. It is estimated that billions of marbles were made. These are the most commonly-found marbles on beaches. Perhaps children took them on holiday and raced them down sand dunes, or tried to skim them on the water? They were also widely used as ammunition for sling shots. Children would set up their targets and shoot at them with marbles. They were also likely to have been discarded at coastal dumps once children had outgrown them. Either way, they have ended up in the oceans for us to find all these years later. They are often a little misshapen after many years in the sea being tumbled and frosted by the tide.

CLAY MARBLE ☐

Clay marbles were mass-produced in the 1870s for people to play various games with. They are usually found in their natural tan colour, but they may also be dyed red, blue, brown, green or yellow.

There is a theory that marbles may have been used as ballast for cargo ships. Empty ships were vulnerable in storms, so if the ship didn't have any cargo, something heavy needed to be put into the ship's keel instead, then swapped with real cargo once in port. This ballast would have then been jettisoned. While some people like to believe that marbles may have been used in this way, it is more likely that free materials like sand and rocks were used as ballast. There is another theory that marbles may have been used to roll heavy cargo freight on and off the ships at the port.

Tidal Treasures

GLASS BUTTON ☐

Glass buttons were hugely popular from the 1800s onwards and are a true treasure to find.

SEA BUTTON ☐

Whilst many buttons found on the beach are not precious, they are still an exciting find as they were a little part of somebody's history. These can be made from materials such as: shell, ivory, horn, bone, wood, plastic and rubber.

MILITARY BUTTON ☐

Older military buttons were made from varying metals and were sometimes plated with precious metals. They come from uniforms and feature various symbols such as coats of arms.

MOURNING BUTTON ☐

In 1861 Prince Albert passed away, leaving his wife Queen Victoria in mourning for the rest of her life. During this time she would only wear black mourning jewellery and clothes adorned with mourning buttons made from the gemstone jet. Victorian fashion was influenced by this and many clothes featured mourning buttons made from glass or vulcanite.

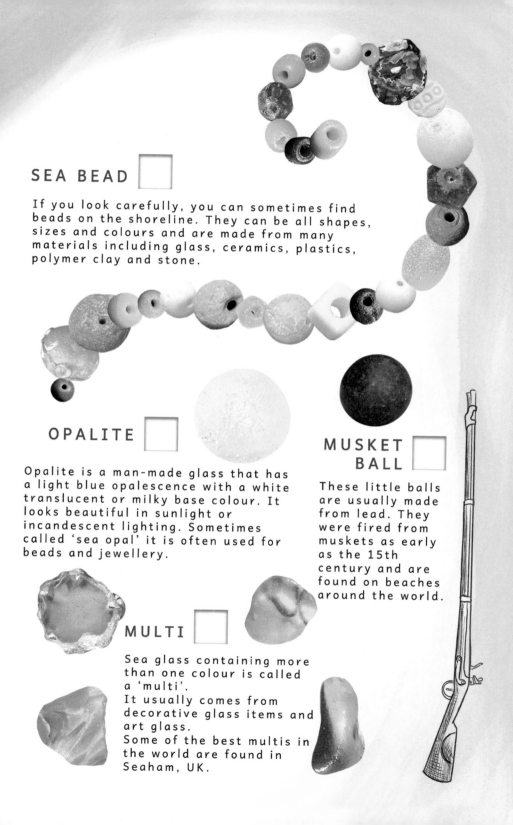

SEA BEAD ☐

If you look carefully, you can sometimes find beads on the shoreline. They can be all shapes, sizes and colours and are made from many materials including glass, ceramics, plastics, polymer clay and stone.

OPALITE ☐

Opalite is a man-made glass that has a light blue opalescence with a white translucent or milky base colour. It looks beautiful in sunlight or incandescent lighting. Sometimes called 'sea opal' it is often used for beads and jewellery.

MUSKET BALL ☐

These little balls are usually made from lead. They were fired from muskets as early as the 15th century and are found on beaches around the world.

MULTI ☐

Sea glass containing more than one colour is called a 'multi'.
It usually comes from decorative glass items and art glass.
Some of the best multis in the world are found in Seaham, UK.

Sea Glass Wonders of the World

SEAHAM MULTI ☐

Seaham Beach in County Durham, UK is famous for beautiful multicoloured sea glass.
From 1853 there was a glass factory called Londonderry Bottleworks, which discarded all its mistakes straight into the sea. People travel from far and wide to this beach for these gorgeous sea jewels.

GERMAN MARBLE ☐

These stunning one-of-a-kind antique cane-cut marbles were handmade in Germany in the early 1800s and are famous for their distinctive swirl patterns. These marbles were individually crafted by skilled glass artisans and can still be found on beaches around the world today.

*There are beaches in the world made
entirely of sea glass! These include;
Sea Glass Beach in Bermuda,
Steklyashka Beach in Russia,
Sea Glass Beach in Okinawa, Japan
and Glass Beach in California, USA.*

JAPANESE OHAJIKE ☐

These little gems look like flattened marbles. They were originally used for a children's game similar to tiddlywinks and are found on beaches in Japan.

MURANO SEA GLASS ☐

This amazing sea glass is found near the famous Murano glassworks in Venice, Italy. The history of glass making in Venice goes back to the 13th century and continues to this day. Most Murano glass is not sea worn, as the lagoon has no surf and no gravel.

DAVENPORT SEA GLASS ☐

Davenport Beach is in California, USA. This amazing sea glass originates from a fine-art glass-blowing company called Lundberg Studios.
It is believed that in the 1970s a huge flood sent containers filled with glass into the ocean.

POTTERY □

Fragments of ceramics come in all shapes and colours.
The best pieces have worn, soft edges.

FIGURINE □

It is always fun to find part of, or even a whole figurine.

MERMAID'S PURSE □

A mermaid's purse is a tough leathery pouch which is an egg case from a shark, skate, ray, catfish or dogfish.

SEA BEAN □

Sea beans are seeds or fruits that originate in exotic countries and are carried into the ocean by rivers and streams. They are also known as 'drift seeds'. Hundreds of different types of sea beans ride the gulf streams, often ending up in Florida.

PIPE STEM □

Pipe remnants can be found on beaches worldwide. In the 16th and 17th century, smoking tobacco using pipes became fashionable. They were made in moulds and were fairly cheap, so were thrown away into rivers and oceans when they stopped working or broke. The stems are most commonly found, but the bowls usually break in the waves. It is very rare to find a whole pipe.

SAND DOLLAR □

Sand dollars are a species of flat burrowing sea urchins, mainly found in temperate and tropical zones.

PIPE BOWL □

Fabulous Finds

HAG STONE ☐

A hag stone is any stone with a natural hole through the middle. They are also known as 'fairy stones'. The hole is caused by sand, or smaller stones grinding into the surface.

FOSSIL ☐

Fossilised sea creatures are found on beaches throughout the world. This example is a pyrite amonite.

COWRIE SHELL ☐

These shells can be found all around the world in different sizes. They were historically used as currency in several parts of the world and are always a joy to find.

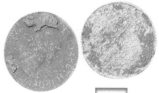

SEA WORN BRICK ☐

Whole terracotta bricks or brick pieces rounded, worn and surf-tumbled.

SEA COIN ☐

Usually the details on coins have been faded by the sea, but sometimes you can see a picture or a date.

METAL TREASURE ☐

Tarnished and faded in the salty water, a metal find often has an interesting back story to research.

SHARK TOOTH ☐

Most shark teeth found on beaches are black or brown and are fossils, but a fresh shark tooth is white. Some sharks can lose up to 50,000 teeth in their lifetime!

Ultimate Sea

COMPLETE COKE BOTTLE ☐

Most sea glass hunters will only ever find pieces of Coca-Cola bottles, but occasionally a whole frosted bottle will be gifted by the tide. Coke bottles vary depending on when they were made and can be over 100 years old!

CARNIVAL GLASS ☐

Carnival glass is pressed or blown multicoloured rainbow-like glass, giving an oil slick effect. It was first produced by spraying metallic salts onto hot glass in the early 1900s as a cheaper alternative to expensive blown irridescent glass. Small chunks of this wonderful glass are a top find for any sea glass hunter.

PIRATE GLASS MARBLE ☐

Sea glass marbles made from pirate glass are rare and beautiful when a light shines through them.

ROYAL RUBY RED SEA GLASS ☐

Red sea glass is extremely rare and was produced by a difficult and expensive process of using gold to achieve the ruby red colour. In 1949, glass manufacturers Anchor Hocking invented a new type of red glass named Royal Ruby, in which the deep red colour was achieved by the addition of copper oxide to the molten glass rather than gold chloride. They produced beer bottles for the Schlitz Brewing Company and occasionally these highly prized Royal Ruby red gems wash up on beaches, mainly on the sands of Puerto Rico.

Glass Gems

GLASS HEART ☐

These decorative little hearts are used as wedding decorations, as gifts or in crafting.
Sometimes they find their way into the sea and are washed up with a beautiful ocean-worn frosted look.

SEA GLASS INSULATOR ☐

Invented in 1844, insulators were installed on telegraph, telephone and power lines to separate the wires from the tall wooden poles and to allow electricity to pass through without interference. They were manufactured between 1875 and 1970. Insulators come in all colours, aqua being the most common.

GLASS DICE ☐

These beautiful vintage dice can be found in many different colours and sizes. They are often tiny, so it is always worth double checking those little pieces in the sand.

GLASS WALKING STICK ☐

Occasionally a section of a twisted glass walking stick finds its way onto the beach.
These canes were used as decorations by Victorians and were sometimes filled with tiny sweets, such as hundreds and thousands. Some believed a glass cane, or 'witch stick' could ward off evil spirits.

Bucket List

FROZEN CHARLOTTE ☐

A Frozen Charlotte is a dream find. It is a small, naked china doll from the Victorian era.
The name comes from a story about a girl called Charlotte who refused to listen to her mother. She was told to put a warm layer over her party dress while she travelled by sleigh to a ball. By the time she arrived she had died from the cold. The moral of the story is, always listen to your mother!
Frozen Charlottes vary in size, the smallest were sometimes baked into Christmas puddings.

MESSAGE IN A BOTTLE ☐

Some beach combers are lucky enough to find a message in a bottle. These exciting finds are wonderful glimpses into history. Some have included desperate messages from shipwrecked sailors, love letters from soldiers, notes from children, scientific experiments charting ocean currents and even a message from a passenger on board RMS Titanic.

WADE WHIMSIES ☐

First developed in the 1950s by Wade Ceramics in the UK. Whimsies were small solid porcelain figures depicting animals and other objects. These tiny figurines were machine moulded and hand painted, creating some unique variations. Originally introduced as a marketing strategy, these figures became extremely popular in the UK and USA and are highly collectable. Occasionally one will get washed up on the beach to be found by a lucky beach comber!

Beach Finds

TOY SOLDIER ☐

Miniature soldiers were used by military strategists to plan battle tactics in the 17th, 18th and 19th centuries. Toy soldiers became widespread during the 18th century, usually made from lead or tin. Modern toy soldiers made from plastic can also be found on beaches.

ARROW HEAD ☐

People have been making tools and weapons out of stones for over 200,000 years. Sometimes these can be found washed up on beaches.
Authentic arrowheads feature flake scars where pieces of the rock were hit away. They are usually made from flint, chert, obsidian, jasper and quartzite.

FISHING FLOAT ☐

Glass floats are a true treasure for sea glass collectors. The most famous of these floats were made by the Japanese, although they were also used in other countries including Korea, Russia, China, Taiwan, Norway and North America.
They were produced in the early 1900s before being replaced by floats made from wood and cork. They were often found washed up on beaches in the 1950s, 1960s and 1970s, but are extremely rare nowadays.

Make a Rainbow!

PRISM OF POTTERY

Ceramic shards come in many
wonderful colours.
Once you have collected enough you
can make a rainbow like this!

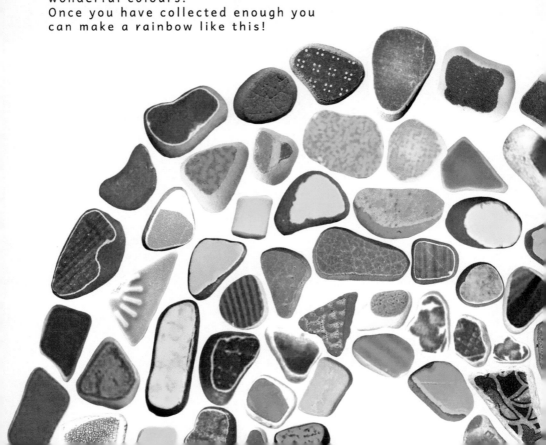

SHIMMERING SEA RAINBOW ☐

Sometimes if you're really lucky, you can find sea glass in every colour, all on the same day!

PERFECT PILE ☐

Balancing a pile of your favourite pieces is called a 'stack'.
This makes a beautiful photo, especially if you can catch it with the sun shining through.

The wonderful thing about sea glass and pottery is that much of it comes from products and packaging, many of which feature logos, brands, words, letters and numbers.
It can take years to build up a full alphabet or a complete number sequence. It is always worth looking closely at those little shards to see if they contain letters or numbers for your collection.

A ☐   B ☐   C ☐   D ☐   E ☐

J ☐   K ☐   L ☐   M ☐   N ☐

S ☐   T ☐   U ☐   V ☐

0 ☐   1 ☐   2 ☐   3 ☐   4 ☐

Find The Alphabet

F ☐ G ☐ H ☐ I ☐

O ☐ P ☐ Q ☐ R ☐

W ☐ X ☐ Y ☐ Z ☐

5 ☐ 6 ☐ 7 ☐ 8 ☐ 9 ☐

Mermaid's Tears

Legend has it...
For hundreds of years mermaids have
been falling in love with sailors.

On stormy nights these sea maidens
have the power to calm the waves,
quiet the winds and lead
ships to safety.

Helping people,
and especially falling in love with them,
is strictly forbidden by Neptune, the god
of the sea. If a mermaid gets caught, she
will be banished to the bottom of the
ocean.

Heartbroken mermaids weep, knowing
they will never see their beloved, or
swim with the ships again.

Their tears wash up on the shores of
beaches in the form of sea glass.
True love, preserved forever as beautiful
ocean jewels.

'Sea Glass Guide'

An original concept by The Wilson Family
© Tapper Wilson Creative Ltd
Written by Lucy, Steve, Holly and Daisy Wilson
Illustrated by Lucy Tapper
First edition 2022

The majority of the photos in this book belong to the Wilson family,
with additional photos kindly donated by fellow sea glassers; Arleen Gonzalez in
Puerto Rico (to see more of her amazing collection check out her Facebook page
"Caribe_SeaGlass by Arleen") Anna Varone in Italy and Jane Kell Cocoran Freeman,
who lives near Seaham, UK. Every care has been taken to include accurate facts and
information, but if you see something that hasn't been included, or is incorrect
please contact us and we will ensure to change it in future printed copies.

**FROMLUCY, STUDIO 3 PIXON COURT, PIXON LANE,
TAVISTOCK, DEVON, UK, PL19 9AZ**

Create your own amazing, unique book to be treasured forever.

www.fromlucy.com

TAPPER
WILSON
CREATIVE
LIMITED

Made in United States
Cleveland, OH
20 November 2024

10737510R00026